You Were Made For This

Finding Courage and Intuition for
Raising a Child with Autism

Written by: Rebecca Jeffreys
Illustrated by: Jeffrey Hoover

Empowerment Publishing & Multi-Media

Copyright (c) 2021 Rebecca Jeffreys. Empowerment Publishing & Multi-Media. All Rights Reserved

Artwork by Jeffrey Hoover

No part of this publication may be reproduced, distributed, or transmitted in any form or by any means, including photocopying, recording or other electronic or mechanical methods, without the prior written permission of the author and/or publisher, except in the case of brief quotations embodied in reviews and certain other non-commercial uses as permitted by copyright law.

ISBN: 9798732627244

Empowerment Publishing & Multi-Media
PO Box 480394
Charlotte, NC 28269
email: admin@epublishyou.com

Disclaimer: This book is designed to provide information and motivation to the reader. It is sold with the understanding that the author is not engaged to render any type of psychological or legal advice. The content is the expression and experience of the author. No warranties or guarantees are expressed or implied. Neither the author nor the publisher shall be liable for any physical, psychological, emotional, financial, or commercial damages, including, but not limited to, special, incidental, consequential, or other damages. Our views and rights are the same: You are responsible for your own choices, actions and results.

Introduction

Yay, **YOU!** for treating yourself to this book! This small investment is the first step to helping you find your power and heart for parenting. I am delighted to share with you my adventure and misadventures in parenting in hopes that it can be helpful for your journey. As I traveled down my road, I was helped along by some many people. I'm fortunate to have a husband who has held me up all the way and supported my parenting style. We were able to access our intuition and trust each other completely. I also learned along the way that it's important to do research and to ask for help. The phrase that "It takes a village to raise a child" is even more profound when your child has special needs. As I built my team of supportive people, my heart burst with love, courage, and happiness. I wish the same for you. As an ASD (autism spectrum disorder) parent you will be challenged to stay in touch with yourself, your identity, your boundaries, your intuition and your emotions. My wish for you is that this book reminds and guides you how to identify your skills and discover that you really are a great parent.

This book can be read cover to cover, or you can pick a chapter as needed. The back of the book offers a glossary of words you will encounter as an ASD parent and pointers for choosing a special education school. For current and up to date resources that I can recommend, visit my website:

www.sproutinghealthyfamilies.com

I'd like to express gratitude for the people who have helped me survive thus far. My husband, John, for his endless support and love. My buddy, Judy Nauman, for acting as second mom and treating my son with unconditional love and holding me up when I needed it. John Butruccio, Jr. for helping me find my way to this important work. Lisa Santiago McNeill, my publisher, for her enthusiasm and help to complete this project. Susan Morse for her kind words, her beautiful poetry in chapter 7 and the guidance she has given my son. To Rebecca Hale for our countless conversations about parenting and for her help with the glossary and kind words about this project. Tess Miller for her feedback on my manuscript and for cheering me on! Jeffrey Hoover for sharing his incredible talent as illustrator and endless support for my crazy projects.

Table of Contents

Introduction 3

Chapter 1 "Does he seem normal to you?" 3

Chapter 2 Finding mindfulness, courage and intuition in times of chaos. 29

Chapter 3 The EGO (Everyone Gets One) 39

Chapter 4 Communication Flaws and Other Funny Mishaps ... 57

Chapter 5 Empowerment 71

Chapter 6 Setting Boundaries 79

Chapter 7 Self-Compassion, Self-Care and Perspective Taking 99

Chapter 8 Celebrate! 109

Appendix: 117

Glossary 124

Additional resources: 132

About The Author 133

About The Illustrator 135

Rebecca Jeffreys

You Were Made For This

Rebecca Jeffreys

Chapter 1

"Does he seem normal to you?"

I can remember the day very clearly. A new friend had come to visit. I trusted her completely because she was the best friend of my sister-in-law. I think she felt this too because she had the courage to ask me this question about my son- "Does he seem normal to you?" She had been observing the situation as my son crawled all over me like I was a jungle gym. Since he was born, 3 years earlier, he had to always be in contact with me. Being a new mom, who dotes over her kid and wants to meet his every need, I thought this was normal. He asks, I give. In return I feel needed. Can you guess my answer to her? Of course, he seems normal! It was normal to me and I had no basis of comparison. Other aspects of his personality were so amazing to me that this one "flaw" was not important. He was writing at age 2, speaking before age 1, could put the alphabet and the planets in order also by age 2, and by kindergarten was a full-blown reader and counter. What more could a mom want? I got a sweet, low maintenance brainiac and I was proud of him. And back to the friend who asked the question. She was kind enough to not divulge that she saw problems in our future.

She knew because she was a preschool teacher and a mom who had seen it all!

I continued to live in my little denial bubble getting stepped on, hair pulled, hugged till choking, bruised, touched out. My poor husband was left with a drained, lifeless woman by the time my son finally went to bed. That really leaves nothing for intimacy!

At age 4 we felt brave enough to try preschool. We were new to the area and had been to just a handful of playdates. I HATED playdates!! Talking about birth stories and poopy diapers was not my thing! Besides, my son never played. He stood on my lap, pulled my hair, kissed me and generally never left my side. I couldn't compare developmental notes because my kid was not like their kid. His vocabulary was so advanced that the children didn't have a clue what he was speaking about. Imagine a conversion like this- My son speaking to a friend of similar age- "Jordy had to go down the Jeffreys Tube (no relation by the way) so he could save the warp core from melting down and travel through a wormhole to another dimension." Yes, I admit it. We loved Star Trek and I have no idea if he understood what he said but he sure seemed to! Can you imagine the faces on these kids? I even had adults telling me his vocabulary was too advanced for them. This feedback fed my proud mama ego and I continued to let it get in my way. My kid is smarter than your kid! Boy, what a power trip! But you know what? I eventually learned that intelligence doesn't count for anything if there are no social skills!

Age 4. Preschool. The reports are not good and they are not helpful. We are repeatedly being told he's behaving badly and hugging the other children non-stop, hopping constantly and has no clue about personal space. That's not a problem at home but in school it's a really big problem! We struggled through and honestly I can't remember many of the conversations I had with his teachers. I just know I felt like a victim and a bad mom and that they were picking on him because he was a boy. That was a common theory among many for us with boys. It made us feel better. I left there with my tail between my legs. Many years later, one of the teachers came up to me. I did not remember her but she remembered me and asked about my son. She was super friendly and seemed to have no grudges about his behavior. How much of my misery was self-made? Not once did anyone suggest we get him screened and even his pediatrician was clueless when I told her our issues. Onward!

Hooray! Kindergarten!! We took him for his prescreening. I was terrified. What would they think? Would they see him as odd, or a problem child? Would they recognize his high intellect??? Oh! My obsession! The teacher's aid delivered him back to us and said there were no concerning issues, and he passed the academic testing with flying colors. I tell you I floated out of there! We were going to be superstars!! Smartest kid in the school and best mom ever!!!

And then we had our first day of kindergarten. He took the bus in and I was free! A whole 6 hours to myself! We made it through just a few weeks before the phone calls started. My first visit I was expecting to visit with the teacher but instead was met by the principal, vice principal and guidance counselor. Right away I felt deceived. These were the people who shelled out discipline, not people who collaborated for your child's success. The meeting was held in a dark, windowless room that felt like a cell. Honestly, I don't remember most of what they said but it was the first time I really had heard the words that my son was different, really different, and I lost it. When I started crying, they asked why I was crying. Well, dumbass, you just made me face a reality that I didn't want. My child is not perfect, and I have no clue what to do. And yet again, no suggestion of a screening made by the school.

During the summer, I expressed my schooling concerns to another mom. She asked me if I had considered another school. Honestly that never entered my head- that's how conditioned I was to only considering public school. She recommended a local Waldorf School. This educational style was developed by Rudolph Steiner (1861-1925) who saw a need for better schools for the children of workers at the Waldorf-Astoria cigarette factory in Stuttgart, Germany. He was inspired to keep the children in nature, let learning blossom at its own speed and center the curriculum around the seasons and special holidays. So I decided to check out our local Waldorf school. One visit to this beautiful school in the woods with calming nature-centered classrooms and I was sold. We decided that since public kindergarten was such a nightmare, we would repeat it and give him an opportunity to have a positive kindergarten experience. This was a fantastic year- still with some struggles- but he was allowed to be himself. Then we began grade one and big changes happened.

His anxiety levels were sky high, he was distracted in class, his social skills were weak. But yet again, despite his struggles, we were determined to keep him in school. That's what you do! Well, this seemed like an obvious solution, so we clamored on. My dreams of having time to myself were once again dashed when we entered grade 1. I had to stay by the phone in case they needed me to come to school to aid him. And they often did. It became such a frequent occurrence that I started staying at a friend's house near the school. We struggled with this plan until it didn't work anymore. Remember at this point we still had no diagnosis. I had plenty of people tell me things that sounded crazy like he has leaky gut or needs craniosacral adjustment, or he has post-traumatic stress disorder from birth or I should take him to the hospital and ask them to figure him out. Things got increasingly worse as he aged. He was hitting his head over small mistakes, strangling his classmates, (he thought it was hugging), and basically scaring the kids and their parents. The school was trying to help by providing a quiet space for him or letting him be dismissed from the room, but nothing was really working. I had come up against the only real flaw at the school, but it was a big one. They were not equipped to handle a boy like mine. To make matters worse, families were filing complaints and we were feeling ostracized and unsupported by the population. In our final meeting with the school, we agreed to take him to see a neurologist. Now, this made sense to me.

It took months to get an appointment. After all the waiting and suffering we were told he does not have autism but we should do the following: horseback riding, social skills classes, occupational therapy and homeschool. After years of struggling with school settings, hearing a medical professional say we should homeschool was the permission we needed. Even though this decision went against the grain of what usually happened in our family, which is full of public school teachers, we embraced it. It was about time I realized that being a rule follower and a mainstream kind of gal wasn't working and that I needed to step outside of my comfort zone to best serve my son. I was surprised and delighted by people's response to this news. They were cheering me on and telling me that I knew what to do! All the fear I built up around this decision was self-made. Finally, I felt courage to do what I felt was right and to listen to what my intuition was telling me. The message had been there all along but I was too stubborn to listen to it.

Deciding to homeschool him was life changing for us. Immediately his anxiety lessened. Since he was a fast learner we completed our school work in half a day so he had plenty of time to just be a kid. During the learning hours he was free to self-regulate sensory issues by swinging in a hammock, sitting in a bean bag chair, standing as needed, snacking as needed, and resting. The pressures to copy the teacher's work (which he would try to do with exact precision) were lessening. It took him a while to embrace his own handwriting (which was not like what he saw in school or printed materials). He could also access a keyboard which was vital due to his weak pencil grip.

Homeschooling did not come instinctively to me and I was terrified. However, the one thing I knew in my heart was that I had to help him feel successful. One of the best suggestions we were given was to take him to occupational therapy (OT). This was so eye opening for us! A huge number of the struggles we had been working with were being addressed here. He would work with a therapist one day a week and we would practice during the week. By far his favorite tool was the rollers. These are two spongy rollers that he could squeeze himself between for deep pressure. Many of the tools at occupational therapy were founded by autism expert, Temple Grandin. She discovered the rollers for herself as a child and later used it in her designs to reduce stress in cow herding! By giving my son deep pressure, we could release stress and anxiety, and in turn, reduce his need for constant hugging. Things were getting easier at home.

By now, I was starting to feel empowered and courageous. I could take the skills I learned at OT and incorporate them at home. As my stress level cooled off and he leveled out, I had enough head space for intuition. Once my intuition turned on, I found my courage and I was able to proceed with confidence in my decisions for him. I even gained more confidence in my teaching style and noticed schooling opportunities presented themselves to us every day. It turns out that the people who said I would know what to do, were right. I just had to find the courage to take my own path, listen to my heart and follow through on what I knew was right for our family.

This was when I finally found my intuition. I no longer had other moms judging me or teachers trying to guide me. I had my head and my heart and they were finally speaking to each other. My teaching genes rose to the top and I was in my element. We had a grand time exploring American History by visiting Concord, Massachusetts and studying geology in Central New York and Canada. How about a trip to England for medieval history? Or Physics classes at Legoland California? We did it! We did schoolwork at home too. This part initially terrified me. I was so afraid I was going to do it incorrectly. I couldn't use a prefab curriculum because his skill sets were beyond his years so I had to devise one for him. We combined grade 3 and 4 into one year. And the same with grade 5 and 6. But his academic work was closer to grade 10. At the end of each year, I submitted samples of his work and signed off on my paperwork for the school system. All was peachy! We had time for school and therapeutic horseback riding and social skills classes and appointments with doctors. The three of us were invincible and I was confident that I was finally being a great parent.

Rebecca Jeffreys

By the time he reached age 12 he was done with being without classmates. He advocated for himself and asked to go back to public school. We scheduled a visit and a meeting and by the end of the day he was registered. Within a week, the school asked me to consider getting him an individualized education plan (IEP). This was unheard of! The school was giving us a gift! They devised his plan, and we had our first meeting. Unlike my previous public-school experience, I was told ahead of time who to expect to be present. We met around a large table and the atmosphere was completely different. This time we were working as a team to help him succeed. One of their requests was that we get him a neuropsychological evaluation and they suggested their own doctor. Well, call me paranoid, but I don't like the idea of an in-house doctor as there is too much room for manipulation. So, I called a medical friend for a suggestion and we got JJ scheduled. I waited three months for this appointment. The date was burned into my brain. I knew it would take most of the doctor's day too. I had set aside the day for us and planned my son's snacks and my activities for waiting, and then about a week before the appointment, the doctor called and said, where are you? What??? I was so confused! I was off by a whole week!!! I was so mortified.

What a failure I was! Now we would have to wait another 3 months to get in and I wasted this doctor's time. My stomach was in knots for days. (Can you hear my perfectionism here?) Well, we eventually had our evaluation done. The results were fascinating but not surprising. He's super smart. Check! And has a fragile ego, social phobia and depression but no autism. I reported back to his new school, and they were disappointed. Here's why they wanted that diagnosis. Money and services. For the school to be able to provide, which they must do by law, they need money for specialists. However, our doctor did give us enough to proceed on. We had severe anxiety disorder and social anxiety as a diagnosis and that's what we worked with until he turned 20. The IEP at the junior high school was effective enough for him to succeed but their best tool kit was the social help. By the end of his 2 years there, he had made a lasting group of friends and he's in touch with them still today! Honestly, I couldn't care less about the academics. The friend part is the real prize! As a teacher and an academic, I never in a million years would have expected to hear myself say academics were not the most important part of school. It's really quite liberating!

Rebecca Jeffreys

If only my personal attitude about academics could have been carried into public high school. Unfortunately, in the state of Massachusetts, students are required to pass standardized tests in order to graduate. That puts a ton of strain on the teachers and students. As a result, high school is all about academics. My son entered grade nine with his IEP in place. We tried to accommodate his need for a tablet, we found a way to provide him an escape route when he was over-stimulated, and we had meetings with all the appropriate teachers. His first quarter, he did surprisingly well considering he had to change classes with the halls filled with 1000+ students. We were able to keep up with homework and we decided to do morning drop off instead of the bus to alleviate that stressor. His grades were quite acceptable but the Special Education Department (SPED) was not really providing any services. They basically decided that unless he was floundering they could ignore him. Then the second quarter started. We were supposed to receive a progress report from the SPED Dept but it never showed up. Honestly, they wouldn't have had anything to say because they were not keeping tabs on him. By November, my son was really starting to show signs of stress. I started reaching out to his point of contact to make alternative plans for him. We were meeting weekly for a while to come up with solutions to help him perform better. One solution was for part of the day to be spent in the SPED room which was quieter. The other was to let him enter the hallways at class changing times a few minutes before the crowds entered. We had also arranged for him to visit the guidance counselor office whenever needed. It seemed like we were all on the same page and supports were in place. And then all hell broke loose. A teacher had noticed he was agitated and decided to escort him to the SPED room. On the way there something triggered him (they had been notified that this could happen) and he shoved the teacher. At the time my son barely weighed 100 pounds. The teacher was fine and did not make a fuss but the school decided it had to follow-through on its blanket rules of "no shoving the teachers or you get suspended."

I tried to be an adult about this and be on the "adult team" but I was furious. I was at a total loss as to how to proceed and I wasn't listening to the little voice in my head saying I should contest it. Instead, I did what was easy and brought him home to be with me, without the stress of school for either of us. I can't say that was the best solution. My son's heart, self-esteem, confidence and interest in school were destroyed by the one action that the school took and I let it happen. We managed to get through the week. He was afraid I was going to "punish him" but that's not my method, plus I couldn't punish him for being him. He was trying to communicate with the teachers but they failed to see that. Besides, he was being hard enough on himself. I took him to meet with his assigned tutor (they had to provide that by law) but it was a huge waste of time and only a gesture on their part. I hated seeing my son go through this.

The week finished and he returned to school and I returned to weekly meetings with the "team." After being visibly shaken by the meeting, one of the special education teachers told me surreptitiously that I could ask for an assistant for him which I did. (Why is everything kept from the parents???) They also yet again requested we get another neuropsychological exam. (which are very expensive by the way) We did this and got a horrible diagnosis which did not align with what I know about my son. I left the appointment in tears and disbelief and with some attitude. This was the moment I finally found courage and decided it was time to make some serious changes for my son.

The doctor had asked for my son's quarterly school reports to which I replied "what reports?" The school was not in compliance in their responsibility to report. Directly from the appointment I went right to the school and asked for the reports. That surprised them because I had been way too passive up to that point. They did a ton of back pedaling and made promises. Eventually, by January, I got my reports.

So the next "team" meeting, which happened in December, I arrived with my evaluation from the neuropsychological evaluation and informed them that they could not provide for my son and we needed to send him elsewhere. This is when they got really creative and "tried" him out in different settings. They tried a hybrid model of some integration and some special education room. Fail. Then they tried full-time SPED room with no academic teacher for him. The special education teacher was busy with the academically challenged students. He was given his work and told to just do it. SUPER fail! By this time, I was really losing it. No academic work was being accomplished and his social emotional needs were ignored. I was a blubbering, crying, swearing mess in the meetings. I'm pretty sure I had a record so in order to not make a HUGE mistake I hired an advocate to help out.

We attended the next meeting together and I felt some of the pressure removed from me. In my fantasy world, she was going to give them attitude and put them in their place and point out their wrongs. And I would sit there smugly watching. Unfortunately that was not her method. She was all about collaboration and finding solutions and hugging. Blech. I needed change NOW! She brought up the suspension and got it removed from his record. Thank you. Then they made more plans, and we scheduled another meeting. Good thing I did not have a day job at the time! After each meeting the advocate and I would have a powwow in the parking lot. I expressed my frustrations with our snail's pace and she said, "Don't worry. Your son will lose it and then they'll understand what we are saying." What? We have to wait for a crisis? That was the dumbest strategy ever! But, she was right and the very next day the school called to say they had good news! My son would be released to another school and he could come home. I jumped for joy! The crisis did indeed happen. They had pushed him over the edge, and he lost it. I felt terrible that it played out like this. It didn't have to.

True to my son's nature when I picked him up he thought I was going to be mad at him. As soon as we were out of earshot of the school, I whooped with joy and hugged him! We were free!! He never had to step in that school again. As luck would have it we were just about to enter a long string of snow storms followed by Christmas vacation and then more snow. As a result he got a super long break and was able to decompress and recover from the whole ordeal. During those days we researched schools and set visiting dates. After selecting a new school and getting paperwork in place, he headed off to his new school in March.

    I could spend the rest of the book telling you all the details of high school, but I won't. I will tell you that he was in the most amazing place. He was loved and supported and learned the important stuff like social and life skills. He was doing great with his academics and he looked forward to school each day. He passed his standardized tests with flying colors and even took the SAT. Each day he brought home enthusiastic stories about his teachers and what he learned. His favorite teacher was his art teacher who encouraged his creativeness. He got his driver's license and even drove the 45 minute trip to school one day (with me on board). The most typical kid moment we saw in him was when we went to the prom! He wore a suit and had a date and rode in a limo. That was one event I had pretty much accepted would not be a reality for him so I was overjoyed when this came to fruition. We saw a happy young man emerge from this positive experience. None of the extreme suggestions made by the neuropsychological doctor were needed. I'm so glad I finally followed my own intuition and fought for what he really needed. My hope for you is that you can see how important listening to your gut really is!

(Helpful tip: Check the index for guidelines for selecting a special needs school.)

"Do I have to move out now?"

Adult life is hard. It's hard for typical people. The carefree days are behind you, you have to focus on making money and paying bills. Feeding yourself and being responsible are so much harder when you enter the adult world. No longer is anyone holding your hand or cooking for you, or cleaning for you. It's a big step and usually a stressful but manageable one. In the autism world the adult defining age of 18 can look completely different. Often, the emotional development can be as far as 7 years behind their peers. This doesn't even count for those who struggle with academic disabilities too.

When I heard this question about moving out from my son, my heart broke. It never occurred to me that he would be told this information by his friends. In my head I thought we made it super clear to him that he was not expected to move out for a very long time. So, for that reason, I felt I had failed him and made unnecessary stress for him. He had been worrying about this for many months and finally asked the morning of his 18th birthday. His dad and I had realized many years earlier that the traditional exit point for our son would come much later than many of his peers. We took this into consideration when it came to our savings and our plans for retirement. Or so it seemed we were totally prepared to help this young person develop into an adult but the world was really not ready to embrace him or any other people with autism.

Before he left high school, we had participated in the required transition meeting. We agreed that he would be capable enough to handle community college and could even drive himself there. All of us felt we were on track and things were bright and shiny. So we followed our plan but there were some unforeseen circumstances. To start with, the supports put in place for him at the college were not enough. He was pretty much expected to act as a typical student and be autonomous. He also never quite understood the grading systems and always figured he was failing. It was becoming clear that we asked him to take on way too much. Three quarters of the way through, he dropped all classes but art. We were all disappointed and feeling like we had failed but we also saw numerous successes. For instance, he did drive himself to school for a semester. He advocated for himself to his parents in expressing his stress level and his concern for keeping his mental health in a good state. And he finished his art class with great success and much praise from his teacher. But now we were without a plan.

My husband and I started some research into gap year programs and found one 45 minutes from our house. Since our savings for college were now not being used, we figured we could slip that right into this option. So, in January he moved into an apartment with 3 other young men. They had to clean and cook for themselves and drive themselves to their internship 4 days a week. The fifth day was classroom work around life skills, mental health and job skills. Some of this worked really well for our son and some of it was a nightmare. By the end of the 3 months, he was done. He had run out of resilience and his perspective was very negative. Even though we worked with the program directors and therapists, we had hit a wall. He was coming home early. Once again, we could feel as if we failed. We probably expected too much too soon but there were numerous successes here too. He drove himself to work daily. He never missed a meeting. He took care of his hygiene and meals on his own and he learned what it's like to share an apartment. Adulting was happening!

In the 3 years following we had some unexpected but helpful changes. He had been exploring metalworking. We signed him up for a class with a jeweler that we knew. As it turned out, my son is quite good at manipulating fine metal and stones into beautiful pieces of jewelry! Finally, we had hit on something that made him feel successful.

At age 20 we had another neuropsychological test done. This time he was diagnosed with autism. The labeling had changed but also, we used a different doctor who had a different take on my son. The diagnosis was exactly what we really needed when he left high school. With the diagnosis, we have been able to work with The Department of Developmental Services and Work Opportunities Unlimited. Both have been fantastic at goal setting, job training and helping him find a job as a bench jeweler. We are now also eligible for Supplemental Social Security, a special needs trust, housing and more. The big lesson we learned here is that we had to reconsider conditioned thoughts about our child's future.

Being flexible and embracing the circumstances with love, joy and support brings about success in unexpected ways.

Deep Dive:

What actions can you take to help your child succeed at school?
Where can you identify successful moments in your parenting?
Can you see how your child's small successes all add up to the bigger picture?
Can you see how a change in perspective and being flexible (ie- shifting a goal) can be the best answer?
Final thought:

I invite you to revisit your conditioned thoughts about education and child rearing. I've been witnessing a slow shift in parents' philosophy about how our children are schooled and they are starting to think differently than what's always been done. Do you have the courage to follow your heart and go against what you've always been told was correct? I want you to know that you are and always will be your child's best teacher. Follow your heart and you will do it right!

You Were Made For This

Chapter 2
Finding mindfulness, courage and intuition in times of chaos

"You've always had the power my dear, you just had to learn it for yourself." Glenda the Good Witch.

If there is only one chapter to read in this book, it's this one. My big goal for moms is to help them understand that they have the courage, intuition and power to be their own leaders. Just as Dorothy from the *Wizard of OZ* was full of doubt, you will be too, but really the answers are inside of you. There's just so much noise, confusion, outside pressure, inner expectations, self-doubt and fear that we lose the power to obtain insight and intuition when it comes to parenting.

We've all had moments when we wished someone would just tell us what to do. We might be hoping for Daddy or Prince Charming or our Moms to fix things when in reality you have the power to fix the things on your own. The part that is missing is courage. Take a minute to think about a time when you knew the answer but you let fear interfere. I can tell you numerous moments when I made career choices or life choices based on what I thought others would think. Who does that help? Well, it may demonstrate to others that I understand a moral compass or it might show that I feel an obligation to others or that I don't trust my own decisions. Depending on the situation it has been all of these! There is a huge assumption made when these rules are applied to our decisions and that other people really care that much about our business. Well, they don't. Just like you, they are wrapped up in their own problems. Unless your decision has dire consequences for them, they honestly will not care. This is not a negative, selfish human quality. It is a self-protective device built into all of us. If we tried to spend energy on everyone else's problems, we would become the problem. (don't be in everyone's business!)

How does this apply to parenting?

No two (2) family situations are alike. This is why you were not handed a "how to" guide when you gave birth. There are just too many variables. So, who's in charge of making family decisions? You and whoever you share the duties with. You get to determine systems for the household, you get to set the rules, you get to be the teachers, the nurses, the therapists, the taxi drivers, the chefs and the cleaning staff. You're in charge and as a result you are empowered to make decisions. Are you worried you might "do it wrong?" Trust me, you will! Parenting and perfectionism do not go together. You will make mistakes and fix mistakes and you will also make glorious successes! So where do we find the answers? In our hearts and heads. It's all there! Just because you have a special needs kid does not mean you are powerless. You are a powerhouse of knowledge and just need to tap into it.

My first courageous move should have happened in kindergarten. Instead of fighting with the school (this school would suspend kindergarteners by the way), I should have pulled him out. The urge to do what was expected of me was overwhelming. Every family puts their kid in school at this age and every family has complaints about their school. This was just normal, right? Well, not really. It was not normal at all and I should never have settled for it. We tolerated it even though it was not meeting our image of kindergarten. My lack of courage ultimately was a detriment to my son.

So how do you get to this inner knowledge?

Mindful Moment, Mindful Intuition

I'm not always good at maintaining an open, receiving mind. One morning as I was brushing my teeth and making my bed at the same time, my brain pointed out to me that I was not in the present moment. I was rushing around getting ready for my day and trying to decide where to start. As I did more chores, it became clear to me that writing was my starting place. Being mindful is a daily challenge for most of us. I was first made keenly aware of how much I needed this practice when I attended Thich (Thay) Nhat Hanh's Buddhist ashram in New York. We started with 2 hours of meditation and singing which was wonderful. (I may have napped) Then Thay appeared and spoke for a couple of hours. Honestly, I don't remember what he said but what happened after he spoke was my cathartic moment. We were all invited for a mindfulness walk. (At this time in my life I was being pulled in numerous directions as a mom and musician. I was constantly running behind and never present for anything as I worried about the next thing in my day.- sound familiar?) We lined up single file behind the monks who then led us around the grounds at a pace they established. Step, pause, step, pause... I thought I was going to die. My heart was racing. It was all I could do to not run past them. This was torture, not mindfulness! I did not know where to look, how to keep my balance, my focus was on my body's unfamiliarity with the slower pace and my stomach felt uneasy. I held my breath until finally we finished. Big sigh of relief. After the walk, we shared a meal together and we were instructed to wash our own dishes. And, in Thay's words, make washing the dishes the most wonderful moment of the day. What...? Dishes?

Spring forward about 10 years. I still learn from these lessons. I actually love washing the dishes. The sound of the water, the way the dirt rinses away, the feeling of accomplishment at the end. I can actually be present here! And concerning the walking meditation, my dog taught me how to embrace this! He's the most zen being I've ever met. Step, sniff, step, sniff, step, sit. "Come, Mom! It's time to sit and enjoy this moment." Our walks are regularly interrupted by resting and observing. Observing! That's what was missing. On my walk with the monks, I did not take any time to observe my surroundings. I was in a beautiful forest, in silence with hundreds of other humans, all seeking answers and I was missing it. Now, thanks to Rigby, I can take the time to observe my surroundings, I can listen to the songs my footfalls make, I can be aware of my breath and I can know, in that present moment, that all that is expected of me is to be present. That's all your child wants too.

So, what does <u>this</u> have to do with parenting? Everything. Find time to be mindful, whether it's a slow walk, meditation, watching incense burn or even closing your eyes for a few minutes to restore yourself. A restored mind has a better perspective, can make rational decisions and choose love over anger. It can help diffuse the frustrations of parenting. Being present and mindful can help you be an observer instead of a reactor. And that alone will help you find intuitive answers to parenting challenges. Autism does not present in traditional ways. Behaviors can be erratic, baffling and frustrating, but a calm mind can help you understand the situation with love and patience and everyone benefits from this type of mindfulness. In time you will become your own leader and guide yourself and family in the best way that fits your situation.

How to be mindful in a stressful parenting moment and make room for intuition:

After ensuring your child is safe…

1. Observe- Look for environmental triggers such as bright lights, temperature changes, smells, loud noises…
2. Take a moment to think and breathe.
3. Ask yourself questions such as "is what they say they need really the solution or perhaps the only words they can think of at the moment?"
4. Did something happen earlier that is arising as a stressor now?
5. Did you make an assumption in your communication and leave out key components that left room for them to draw an incorrect conclusion?
6. Have you, or they, forgotten to bring along a favorite calming item such as a stuffed animal, book or fidget toy?
7. Are they struggling to transition to the next activity?
8. Did you give them a chance to express their wants or did you just boss them around? Did you empower them?

9. Did you invalidate their feelings?
10. Practice saying the mantra- "It's only temporary" to help you keep perspective.
11. Then address the problem with the solution you have acquired. This will get easier as you trust your gut more and learn your child's communication skill.

The important part here is to ask yourself questions. The answer will come if you are quiet enough in head and heart. Be an observer instead of a reactor.

Rebecca Jeffreys

You Were Made For This

Chapter 3
The EGO (Everyone Gets One)
Removing guilt, blame, shame, and perfectionism

It took 2 years before we were able to conceive. We went through fertility therapies but all that did was run us down. Once we stopped trying so hard, our son was conceived much to the surprise of all of us since my ability to conceive without medical help was considered "unlikely." As you can imagine the joy of learning we were pregnant was overwhelming, but I immediately started wondering if I had done something wrong already. Because of my particular circumstances I was 3 months along when I learned I was pregnant. So along with excitement came self-doubt and fear. Did I eat something I shouldn't have? Did I take too many Tylenols? Did I get exposed to toxic chemicals? It was a long list of events I tried to remember to be sure I did not mess up the first trimester. Shortly thereafter I had a test done that alerted my doctor to the potential of a birth defect. Talk about scary! And so the blame game began. I blamed my doctor, I blamed myself, I blamed my job, my body. I was convinced I had already failed. Fortunately a second test revealed that the first test was wrong and we had misjudged the age of the baby. What a relief. With that behind us I spent the rest of my pregnancy in maternal bliss and anticipation. All was unfolding as it should.

We welcomed our beautiful boy and raised him the best we could as new parents. Which means we worried a lot and tried too hard, but it was all working despite our flaws. My sense of self-blame was long gone until he entered first grade. He was showing obvious behavior problems and his teacher declared that he had autism. I did not give this any credit because, 1) It's not her place to declare this and 2) None of his doctors had alerted us to this. But here's the killer, as I was leaving, visibly upset, she had the nerve to say "Don't blame yourself. It's not your fault." I wanted to give her a few choice words for even suggesting that. By this time, I was a proud parent and full of confidence in my ability to raise this beautiful boy. Her comment felt undermining. I have since learned that there is a history of blaming the moms for children with autism. It was all started by a doctor in the 1940's. Unfortunately, this blame persisted well into the 80's labeling parents as "refrigerator moms" meaning they were cold, neglectful and distant. I find this term repulsive as most moms I know are exactly the opposite and shower their kids with love and attention. Until the teacher's comment reached me, it never occurred to me to blame myself for his symptoms. And I'm glad I did not buy into it. Sadly, I still see people perpetuating this ignorance. In one Facebook group for moms of autism kids, one member posted that her friend would not let her child play with an autistic boy for fear of him catching it. She also believed girls could not be autistic. That moment would have been a great time to educate others but unfortunately the mom's emotions got the best of her and she closed-down and self-protected. I don't think she's alone in that response, but I wish it could have played out differently. I urge <u>you</u> to find the strength to teach others about autism and stop the myths. Not only for you but for all moms and dads with kids with disabilities.

Now that I am 22 years into parenting this young man and our diagnosis did eventually prove to be autism, I have never felt the need to blame myself. My hope for all moms and the moms of the future is that they too value their love for their child and themselves and never blame themselves. You have made a beautiful human and you are a beautiful human. Keep up the good work and keep up the belief in yourself! It's to everyones benefit.

Your Ego and Perfectionism

A man told Gautama Buddha *"I want happiness."* Buddha said, *"First remove "I," that's Ego. Then remove "want," that's Desire. See now, you are left with only "happiness."*

I love this quote. It's one I like to visit pretty regularly. The ego is such a complex system and difficult to understand. However, this quote sums it up for me and reminds me how to become centered again.

Upon reflecting on my earlier years as a competitive musician, I can see how my ego was the boss. I loved outside validation and sought it like a drug. Seeing my name in print in programs and on posters was a cheap thrill. As I matured, I began to find this kind of feedback was no longer necessary. I was recognizing myself for who I was instead of who I thought I should be for everyone else. This was about the time I started craving having a child. I was ready to change my focus away from "I" and what I wanted and instead focus on helping another human being. However this did not mean that my ego just went away. It took work and it took confidence as I matured into mothering. And still the negative side of the ego would still show up.

I've spent many years reading about the ego and trying to better understand it but in reality, I've found it really comes down to identifying what that little voice is telling you about yourself and how you choose to react to it. Every day we make decisions about our behaviors- some are negative, and some are positive. Sometimes the negative choice, the little voice that self-sabotages you, gets your attention and declares itself a winner. When that happens, your ego is trying to take over. The ego really is a self-protective monster. It will build a barrier around you and engulf you to the point where you cannot see clearly. Let me give an example. Pretend you are visiting the newsfeed on Facebook. A friend is boasting about his fabulous son and all of his accomplishments as an athlete and a scholar. What do you feel in your gut? If you are in control of your ego, you celebrate for and with him! But if you've never done ego work before then you most likely feel resentment because your child isn't and won't be like his. So your ego goes into self-protect mode and fills you with negative emotions toward a situation (the other child) who is no threat to your well-being. Now let's take another approach to this. Who gets to decide if you are proud of your child? Society? No. The people on Facebook? No. Your parents? No. The only person who gets this privilege is YOU! If you are feeling shame, where does that come from? Conditioning from your childhood most likely. Do you like that feeling? Do you want to perpetuate it in your household? Probably not! So why do it?

You really do get to choose! The ego loves shame but YOU do not have to. Nor do you have to embrace resentment, embarrassment, hatred or any other negative emotion. Those are all ego based. The parents who impress me the most are the ones who have unlimited pride in their kids who struggle. They don't hide their children's limitations. They celebrate them and their successes. They have thrown out society's scale of success and built their own. Can you see how liberating that is?

By sharing your neurodiverse adventure in the typical world you could be a blessing to others and open them up to celebrating with you. Before you know it you will change the social media landscape into something positive.

How did your ego respond to the autism diagnosis?

Did you see it as a negative reflection on you? Did you let it define you? Did you feel blame, shame, embarrassment or think that you have bad genes? If all of these came up for you, this is your ego talking. This is the part of our bodies who recognizes survival of the fittest. Your ego is telling you that you or partner's breeding is flawed. Your ego will tell you that your deepest imperfections and insecurities are now going public. Your survival instinct will fight to leave behind the flawed child and start anew somewhere else. I know this sounds harsh, but this is eons of programming!

BUT YOU DON'T HAVE TO GIVE INTO THAT!

The good news is that you can choose how to respond to the news of an autism diagnosis. You can get angry and find a place or person to blame, you can run away from your partner and let them deal with it, you can live with shame and never talk about your child, or you can embrace your child and take pride in the gift you have been given. Shame is an emotion that gets assigned to circumstances and it's also an emotion that can be removed. Most shame raises its ugly head because we are afraid what our peers will say. So we self-protect because we think we already know they will think less of us. We assign shame and ignore or berate or vilify the situation just to save face. However, if you show pride, and wonder and acceptance, and if they are people of quality, they will share that with you. There is an old expression, "Shame is a soul eating emotion," by Carl G. Jung that sums up the danger that comes with embracing shame. It's not healthy for you or for use as a parenting tool.

If you have an adult ADS child how does this question make you feel?

"What is your child doing with their life now?"

This question comes up in conversation for me on a regular basis from inquiring people. They are just making conversation but what they don't realize is that my reaction to it is felt in my gut. I feel dread, hopelessness, worry, judgement and I want to avoid answering. The person posing the question is not trying to make me feel this way. I am making me feel this way. I have to ask myself, "where are these feelings coming from? Am I worried they will think less of me as a mother? Am I afraid they will think my son is a slacker? Am I afraid they will then share all the glorious stories about their perfect, typical child?"

Yes, yes, and yes! All of these things come up for me. For the majority of my life, I deceived myself into thinking I could show people what to think about me. I could be accomplished, smart and put together and I'd leave no room for them to find imperfection. My level of control over the world would astonish them and maybe even intimidate and make them feel jealous. Talk about a misdirected power trip!

So here I am back in this conversation and I'm facing my own expectations of how perfect mothering should look. My ego says I should have raised a perfect child, accomplished, put together and powerful. Why? So that I could brag on Facebook and intimidate others with my wonderful mothering and genius child who will save the world? Maybe but that was my ego wanting that. And my ego can often be misdirected. So there are many ways I could handle the dreaded question, but there is only one correct way.

1. I could be aloof and say "he's fine" and leave it at that.
2. I could be defensive and say "Stop asking me that. It's none of your business."
3. I could lie and paint some glorious picture that no human could live up to.
4. I could be up front and proud about my child and exactly where he/she is right now because I know I am doing what's right and that they are trying their very best to do what they need, in their own time.

Can you guess the right answer?

Have you been guilty of numbers 1-3?

Can you see how #4 is so empowering?

#4 takes courage but it's also the right thing to do. I promise you, if you speak with pride about your child, you leave no room for criticism. I have yet to encounter another parent who didn't nod approvingly when I said he's doing A, B, and C and he's healthy and stable. That's all anyone wants for their child. Wellbeing. Wellbeing looks different in every household. A home full of overachieving children can be healthy or it can be full of stress, perfectionism and unreasonable expectations. It really comes down to what your most important core value is for your home. If trophies and ribbons are your only way to measure success, you may want to reconsider some other areas such as compassion, charity, caregiving, responsibility and morals as places to get ribbons and trophies too. Those really are the wins that carry you through life.

So how does my home life look? It's perfect in its imperfection. There's too much screen time (by some people's standards) there's no pushing an agenda on my child, there's support both emotionally and financially, there are services provided for career and emotional growth, there are open listening hearts, there are life lessons taught and modeled, there are shared values and there is love. It's a slower than traditional model of 4 years of college into the job market, but honestly, that model isn't really working anymore anyway. So we let life unfold and we watch him grow into a wonderful adult and we support him. Where that takes him is up to him but we will be here as long as he needs.

"Love isn't a state of perfect caring. It is an active noun like struggle. To love someone is to strive to accept that person exactly the way he or she is, right here and now."   -Mister Rogers

Extra thought about explaining your child's behavior in public:

I bet you can recall a moment when your child embarrassed you in public. It happens to everyone. It could be as simple as them revealing something about your private life or it could be a massive meltdown. Either way, you'll immediately feel stuck between two places: deciding if this is a moment that requires discipline in public or if it's something that can be fixed in the quiet of home. The public disciplining can sometimes happen out of pure frustration or it can happen because you are worried about how you look to your peers. Take a moment to recall when you disciplined your child in public. Was it effective? Did it gain you fans? Did it change the situation for the better? Did you feel better about yourself?

I suspect the answer to these questions is no. So, what can we do to handle these public moments? Go to your intuition tools and forget about the spectators. Use the tools you know that can diffuse the situation. Show your child love by focusing on them and letting go of your ego. No parent can fault you for handling a situation with love and compassion and I even bet a few would nod in understanding because they too have been there.

And a final thought on parenting- It's OK to lose your shit. You are going to. There is no way around it. You are going to get frustrated, your buttons will be pushed, you will be judged, you will be tired and challenged and drained. And you will lose it. No matter how we try to stay under control and choose our emotional reactions, we get pushed over the brink. Your first instinct might be to harm or yell at yourself or another person but this is really when you have to dig deep into your resourcefulness. Recognize that you have been stretched and you are not in a good place to behave rationally. Step back from the situation and reassess. As Pema Chodran, the Buddhist nun, says, "Refrain, Reframe and Relax." My favorite tool for my emotional cool down was my mantra "It's only temporary." If you do lose control, find forgiveness for yourself. Apologize to the other party, if needed, but mostly, be good to you. Guilt, blame and shame are not healing or helpful emotions. Just know that you are among the millions of other parents who have lost control. Welcome to the club.

Deep Dive:

1. List some characteristics about your child that make you very proud. Write a fictional Facebook post based on your real life with your child. Eliminate any judgement or worries about others and celebrate that which brings you joy. Find the courage to brag about your version of normal.

2. Which of your feelings are warning signs that you are nearing exhaustion and about to lose control? Make a note of these so you can address them <u>before</u> you lose control. Just as you work to avoid your child's triggers, you can do the same for yourself.

3. Can you identify some ways that your ego limits your ability to be a better parent? In other words; Do you always have to be the best or perfect? What would happen if you ignored these signals and instead lived your best life without these expectations?

4. Can you think of a moment that you had to be right? Was this a power struggle with another person or your child? How would it feel if you conceded? Would you find strength in knowing you could concede in order to de-escalate a situation and yet keep the knowledge to yourself that you were right? Sometimes giving another person a "win" is exactly what they were seeking.

5. For more exploration into "shame" I invite you to look into Brené Brown's amazing work. I am particularly fond of her book titled *The Gifts of Imperfect Parenting.*

Final thought about the EGO:

You may be wondering if the ego can be a positive part of yourself and yes! It can! A healthy ego can give you a sense of purpose, recognize what you have accomplished on this planet, and instill pride. Pride can be a very positive emotion and one that is not felt enough by autism moms. It's really OK to give yourself a pat on the back and recognize the hard work you are accomplishing. Also recognize your parenting intuition and all the love you can create. You are a being of value and meaning that is worth celebrating. YOU are worthy!

"You may not control all the events that happen to you but, you can decide not to be reduced by them."

- Maya Angelou

Rebecca Jeffreys

You Were Made For This

Chapter 4
Communication Flaws and Other Funny Mishaps

When it comes to making assumptions, we are all guilty of it! Most of the time we don't even know it's happening and then we get more information and realize- oops! We completely misunderstood the situation. As a neurotypical person these mistakes are easy to figure out and correct and move on. Not to say they can't cause damages- many relationships have been destroyed by assumptions. But I want to focus on the neurodiverse mind and how it receives information. Please note: I am not a neuroscientist (maybe in my next life!) but I do love thinking about how the brain works. And I'm coming to you with personal experience of living with a neurodiverse human.

I was 32 when I had my son and considered myself more mature than most moms. So, by the time he reached 7 and we were sitting with a neurologist to figure him out, I allowed myself to get angry at her diagnostic efforts. Of course, she asked us a series of questions (we may have been in denial about a few of those answers!) but then she showed my son some pictures with words under them. They were labeled with things like "Let's hit the sack," or "That's the way the cookie crumbles." He had to choose the picture that matched the phrase. But they wanted the idiomatic answer! He got a few right but mostly he was literal. Meaning the drawing of the crumbling cookie was the right answer according to him. I know I should have extreme respect for this woman who had trained as a neurologist, but I found that assessment tool very flawed and unfair. Being able to understand the drawings required a certain amount of life experience and exposure to idioms that my 7-year-old did not have. When I pointed that out to her she just smiled. Her conclusion was that he did not have autism but he needed therapies. So I left the hospital confused and with a task list "as long as my arm" (another idiom).

So there is another setting that I hate the use of idioms and that is in the news. I don't think reporters realize how much they rely on them. I would say about 95% of the time, I can figure them out but my worry is for the atypical mind. Just take a second to enjoy this crazy idiom filled story and I want you to read it literally!

One day I was taking a walk and I encountered a friend. At the time I was lost in my thoughts so he scared me when he said,

"Penny for your thoughts?" I apologized and let him know I did not have a penny. He waved and said, "A penny saved is a penny earned." I waved back, confused. The next block my school teacher said hello and asked me why my homework was not finished and if I had "Bitten off more than I could chew." I didn't answer as I wondered why she thought I was eating something. My mouth was empty and I was actually heading to the bakery. I passed two people at the gas station. One was saying, "Dang! This fuel costs an arm and a leg" I ran away quickly so as not to witness him paying with his arm and leg. As I took off, I bumped into a stranger who said "Better put up your hood. It's gonna rain cats and dogs." What?? I ran as fast as I could to the bakery before they landed on me. When I arrived in the shop the owner greeted me with "Why you must be fit as a fiddle to run that fast." She's obviously confused because people are not fiddles. I looked at the pastry case and thought carefully about my choice. Before I could place my order she said "Girl, you've got your head in the clouds." I did not see any clouds. I asked for the price of the lemon cookies and she said "They were a dime a dozen. Why not try something more special? These are the best things since sliced bread. And I'll let the cat out of the bag, my donuts have a special ingredient. Come on, spill the beans and tell me what you want. Throw caution to the wind." I looked her in the eye and said, "Where are the beans so I can spill them?" She laughed! I replied, "I'm ready to choose." I took my pastry and turned away. She said, "Wait, you have to pay me. Money doesn't grow on trees!"

Obviously, all of these people are well versed in idioms except for the narrator. You might understand exactly what's happening here, but the atypical mind does not. Can you imagine if someone told you cats and dogs were going to rain down on you and you thought that was an actual fact?

So if idioms are so difficult for a neurodiverse mind the solution is simple. Just be literal. Avoid poetic phrases and euphemisms that unnecessarily embellish what you are trying to say. It's really that simple. If you like to listen to the news or read books with your child, point out phrases to them that may be nebulous or confusing or could be completely misconstrued. Take time to explain them. This way you are empowering them to embrace the American language which is laced with suppositions and nonliteral language.

If idioms present a challenge, what about sarcasm? Sarcasm is defined in Merriam's dictionary as ironic wit meant to hurt another individual. If that is the case, why do we ever use sarcasm? Sarcasm has been used for far more circumstances than to direct hurt. I'd say its most popular use is to convey humor and it is completely dependent on context. Let's take this example.

You finished first in a race and everyone is celebrating. Your coach draws attention to you and says, "Maybe someday you'll learn how to run!" Of course, this is meant as a silly way to deliver a compliment, but it may not be perceived that way. Most humans can decipher sarcasm by their early teens. Teachers start to use sarcasm in the classroom (often without realizing it) to bring levity. Parents use it to offer what they feel is a fun way to boost their method of giving praise. But remember what I said earlier about living with a literal mind? Go back to that first phrase and hear it literally. You have just one a race, you feel confident and accomplished and someone accuses you of not knowing how to run. How confusing is that? Talk about deflating them instantly!

Another example: A student who is not confident about their drawing skills gets special mention in a gallery. In an effort to use irony and sarcasm you say "Who is this terrible artist?" You are expecting the artist to smile and beam with pride, understanding that you mean just the opposite, but the literal thinker will be just that- literal, heartbroken, and any level of lack of confidence is going to destroy their sense of accomplishment.

Can you see how harmful sarcasm can be when used at the wrong time? When is the right time? Well unfortunately, not everyone will know when it's right and it will be different for everyone. Some people will never grasp it. As I mentioned earlier, typical teens start to grasp it in junior high school, but others won't. And the atypical mind may take even longer. In order to clarify and speed up this method of communication it must be explained and practiced. Don't be afraid to ask your child "do you know what they really mean?" when you hear someone use sarcasm. Your child may even enjoy learning about this as a technique they can practice and employ. I have found this a good time to teach irony as well.

One young adult that I've worked with would point out to us when they had heard sarcasm or irony. If you are a fan of Sheldon Cooper in the Big Bang Theory you will observe his hilarious attempts to identify and understand sarcasm. If you like to read aloud to your child, point out the moments of irony and sarcasm and explain them. And if they love to write stories, they can learn how to employ these techniques as well!

Mind the Gap!

This expression originates from England and refers to the gap between the platform and the underground train called the Tube. When you get on the train a voice says, "Mind the gap!" to make sure you don't fall in between the train and the platform. It's a funny expression that makes sense in context. Now that you are a parent of an autistic child, I want to encourage you to mind a different kind of gap. Language requires an innate skill of inferring or filling in the gaps. We all naturally leave out details that we deem inconsequential or obvious. Unfortunately, the autistic mind often needs all of these micro details to piece together the whole picture. This can be an exhausting way to speak to someone but it's really quite important. When I finally realized this truth, it made me feel so uncomfortable, like I was condescending to him. In reality it was exactly what he needed and craved.

Taking communication for granted has resulted in some very funny situations in our home. So much of human communication is implied, meaning we expect the other party to fill in the gaps. For instance, if you were to ask your partner to take out the trash, you expect them to take a bag of trash from the kitchen and put it in the can in the garage or whatever system you have devised. Naturally, you take some of the instructions for granted. But imagine if those details are not filled in by one's mind. "Take out the trash" can mean anything! It could mean, take your own personal trash can and put it outside. Well, that's baffling. But OK. Mom said so! Or it could mean, take the bag out of the kitchen can and place it next to the can on the floor. Or, it could mean take out the whole can, trash and all! To you or I this did not seem ambiguous but to the autistic mind it's completely ambiguous! Clearly, more than half of the instructions are missing.

I work with a speech therapist whose whole philosophy requires slow speaking and explaining of everything. I wish I had this technique when my son was younger! I never realized how much I take for granted that the person I'm speaking with can infer and fill in the blanks. Additionally, I expected every person to process information at the same speed which is not true at all. Here's a perfect example- We were on vacation and we decided to visit a very famous gorge in central New York. We had informed our son that this was going to happen. He was excited and the trip to get there was uneventful, but as soon as we arrived it started "going downhill" (another idiom). He was agitated and confused. Despite his behavior, we bought our tickets and waited for the boat to pick us up. This attraction required riding in a boat through a cave system. My husband and I were both in our own little worlds of childlike wonder while my son was silently freaking out. He made it through the ride, but he was pretty angry when we finished. It was not anything like he imagined. He thought we would be walking into caves and through gorges and that it was just a natural outdoor feature accessible by a trail. It never occurred to me that I'd need to explain this setting because in my head, I knew what we were doing. My poor son had completely different expectations based on previous experiences. I failed to explain to him what the experience would be like. This was actually a great lesson for me because it forced me to think ahead and anticipate possible misunderstandings. By fully explaining what would happen on our next adventure or even during an activity at home, I could stop issues before they started. For some kids this may mean that they even need their routine for the day explained to them or they might need to practice "dinner out" while at home. It's only human that we all fear the unknown but for the autistic mind, fear overwhelms even the simplest of tasks. Often, they can't tell you what is scaring them because it's the lack of knowledge that makes life terrifying. Their best answer to your question, "Why are you so anxious?" really is "I don't know."

Here's another example. You are running late, and your kid is half dressed and you really need them to help you. So, you say, "get your shoes and socks." Therefore, they do just that and nothing more. The socks don't go on the feet, shoes remain off and you've only gained about 30 seconds. When you start to recognize the language breakdown it can become very comical! And that's where I want you to take this. In these moments you have a choice to break down, throw a tantrum and be a mess or you can take a deep breath, laugh about the scenario, fix it and move on. (Trust me, I've had the breakdowns and they accomplish nothing.)

One of the toughest challenges for a person with ASD is reading body language. As it is, most of them make very little eye contact and many have trouble reading facial expressions or even remembering faces. So this style of communication is even harder for them to grasp.

You Were Made For This

If you are a neurotypical person, you can read body language without being taught much about it. A wave, pointing, smiling, or clapping all have universal meanings and it is unlikely your parents had to really explain them. Imagine if those movements of your body meant absolutely nothing to the person you are trying to communicate with. In a time of emergency, raising a hand to say "stop" can be lifesaving. But if the receiving human does not connect with this sign, the results can be disastrous. Conversely, I recently had a funny moment with my son who was waving to me. I thought he wanted me to go in and hug him, so I did- much to his annoyance. What he was really saying was go away. Leave me alone. It was a comical misunderstanding and we both departed with a chuckle. But there is so much more to body language than you may realize. Take a second to think of the silent communication you can understand with any typical person. And now take a minute to think about life without that skill. Can you see how confusing things could get?

You probably rely on these signals every day without realizing it. Take that skill away and you have a deeper understanding of the world your child lives in. I am not a child behaviorist and I can't pretend to know all the techniques to help your child, but I can help you to gain a deeper understanding. I was shocked when my son's school called to say he needed speech therapy. What? He's a walking dictionary! The weakness she saw in him was his inability to understand personal space or to read body language. Without this explanation I would have remained completely confused and been unable to help him at home.

There are numerous other language limitations that can exist such as slow processing speed and apraxia. Be sure to connect with a speech specialist who can help you identify issues. Most of this work will be done in the home setting so it's best to be empowered with tools for success. And the more honest you are with your specialist about challenges and progress, the more success you will have.

You Were Made For This

Chapter 5
Empowerment

Are you helping your child or harming them when you do everything for them? Do you use your "helpfulness" as a way for you to measure your ability to be a good parent? Your method of helping may actually be disempowering your child without you realizing it. Disempowerment is a big word that can refer to so many situations. It's a word that I think really needs to be explored in parenting because I have been guilty of doing this to my child. I know it sounds like I'm admitting to some horrible crime but, in reality, all parents do this out of love even if it is a misguided form of love.

If we break down the word dis-empowerment its meaning becomes clear; To remove one's own or someone else's power. Usually, this word is used to describe a power of self-care or emotion versus some violent self-defense action. I'm sure you can quickly identify times when you disempowered yourself, but are you aware of when you are disempowering your own child?

Moms and dads are love machines. They want what's best for their kids and they want their children's lives to be easier than theirs were. Let me give you a few examples of how we think we are helping our children and showing love…

1. We don't expect them to do chores because "they will have to do that for the rest of their adult lives. Let them be kids!"
2. We conversely say "This is your time to be a student so go study and take copious amounts of extracurricular activities so you can get into college."

(and yet we fail to teach life skills.)

3. You indulge your child's every material request so they can fit in. "Everyone is doing it or has it or needs it."
4. We fail to say "no" because our kids may not like us.
5. We don't listen to our gut and instead we go with the popular stance or the easier route which may really not be the guidance your child was seeking.

So, let me give you an example of where I used to disempower my own son. When our kids are little, we are programmed to feed them and help them. That's our job. But at some point they need to start caring for themselves. I failed to see when that should happen so here is my 7-year-old, who is quite capable of getting himself a glass of water, asking me to get it for him- While he's standing in the kitchen! And what do I do? I get it for him!! I think it was at about this time that my husband started saying, "Let him get it for himself." Well, thank you for that wake-up call. My husband showed me that I needed to break my habit of serving and start empowering. And so for the first time I said to my son, "You can get it yourself." Actually, my son was surprised by this because he didn't know he <u>could</u> do it! And so, a new habit was born. Did he still ask for help with things? Yes, but often I also refused to help. I had to constantly remind myself that I was helping him by not helping him. So, to continue empowering him, I would help less and less especially when I knew it was a task he could handle such as zipping his jacket or packing his lunch box or even doing his laundry.

A few words about the power of chores. Chores are not a punishment. They are an important contribution to the society (your home) in which children live. By doing chores, they are part of a bigger fabric and learn that other people depend on their contribution for the running of the household. Chores also build life skills which are not taught in school. I have a perfect example of the importance of chores. One summer I was a counselor at a residential camp. This camp was an eye opening experience for the campers because for the first time in their lives, in their teen years, they had been asked to do chores. They had to clean toilets, and sweep floors and maintain order in the common spaces. I actually had to teach them how to hold brooms. These girls had no understanding of how to care for their personal spaces or public spaces. It had always been done for them. Because of this they had no concept or appreciation for the hard work people had done for them. Can you see how disempowered and disconnected these kids were?

Really our job as parents is to help our child grow into a self-dependent adult. Notice I'm not using "independent" because that implies, they are fully capable of moving out and living alone. This is not true for every human- especially those with special needs. However, no matter where they end up living as adults they need to have the power to care for themselves, make decisions about their well-being, advocate for themselves and do what makes them happy! These life lessons begin in the home and can begin as early as the child is capable and continue through young adulthood.

I challenge you to notice where you can empower your child. I'm willing to bet that you are doing way more for them than they need. By empowering them, you are encouraging confidence and independence and freeing yourself up for your own self-care. Love=empowerment=love. Power up!

Deep Dive:

1. Name three chores your child can successfully do at home.
2. Determine a schedule and a way to remind and communicate when the task should be done.
3. Offer them praise for a job well done.
4. Pat yourself on the back for having the courage and strength to let go and empower them!

Rebecca Jeffreys

You Were Made For This

Chapter 6
Setting Boundaries

"It's impossible," said pride.
"It's Risky," said experience.
"It's Pointless," said reason.
"Give it a try," whispered the heart.
-Author Unknown

Well, we've discussed empowering your child. Now I want you to empower yourself so you can get your needs met. It's time to set some rules!

Boundaries are necessary and life without them can lead to some very stressful and funny moments. As women, we struggle to understand the importance of boundaries. Right now, at age 54, I'm seeing how important they are. Let's look at how we are conditioned as women:

When we are children, we are instructed to always please other people; Do as told, stay out of the way, follow instructions, stay out of the formal living room, keep our clothes clean, do our chores...

As teens this translates into please the boy or girl you have a crush on, morph yourself into something you are not to get their attention or accepted into a group, give away your free time to homework that will never serve you as an an adult (yep- I said it!), choose your future plans based on other peoples' expectations, kiss (or more) the boy or girl so we won't disappoint them.

Young adults do whatever we need to to please the boss- work late, spy, lie, gossip to get ahead, do demeaning tasks or even succumb to sexual workplace pressure, give away your free time in hopes of getting recognition. Or even get into serious debt to keep up with your peers.

In Married life we let our partner determine our lifestyle, don't communicate about intimate preferences, have more children than you want, hold yourself back as to not overshadow your partner, ride under the radar and not rock the boat.

In parent life we give the kids everything they want, not establishing personal space, never going out on dates with your partner, not establishing events that are just for the parents, including the kids in everything, planning meals only around their tastes, keeping the cartoon network on ad nauseum, never allowing for self-care.

Do you see yourself in any of these moments? I see myself in many and my friends in many. I count myself in the crowd who felt like they were in control until the kids came along. In my mind, I was expected to now give my whole life to my child. I even remember telling my husband to not take it personally if all my attention was on my child. I felt that was my duty. So was I able to follow through on this grand goal of martyrdom? Yes and no. For sure I was focused on the baby, but I eventually recognized that I needed to keep some of my definition too.

Boundary Tip #1 **Inform your family of your emotional needs**

At the time I had my baby I was a musician. I was used to working weekends and traveling for concerts. I had to be honest with myself that I still needed that part of me to remain happy. Here's why this was so important- if you give your whole self over to your child, your empty space will fill with resentment and that doesn't serve anyone. So I chose to keep my favorite music activities. I had one night out a week for rehearsals with my favorite ensemble and every February, I took a weekend away with other musicians attending concerts and classes and teaching. Did I feel guilty? Not one bit. Did my husband resent me? Not a bit. There are many benefits to be had here.

1. I could recognize myself as part of a professional community
2. My husband could experience full-time parenthood
3. My son and husband could bond
4. I could get reinvigorated in my life and have more to talk about than diapers and rashes.

5. I established early the message to my husband and child that I am more than just a mom and that it is important for me to keep the professional part of myself.

Boundary Tip #2 **Give yourself a private space**

Now let's talk about home life. I made a great discovery after I gave birth. I finally admitted to myself that I hated sharing a bathroom! Going into my married life I wanted to share everything because in my head, that's what you do. But after giving birth, I really wanted my privacy. So much of my body had been made public before, during and after birth that I was desperate to have a private space. So, I moved into the guest bathroom. What a difference this made for my psyche! It seems like such an insignificant decision, but it really was a game changer. I could let my guard down and not worry about someone walking in on me or me holding up the bathroom. My hygiene was mine and not public. I had full ownership of my self-care.

Another place that needs to be claimed by parents is the bedroom. I know it can be hard to have intimacy with your partner after children have arrived but it is super important. Afterall, that's the whole reason you united in marriage in the first place. It's OK to admit that! We were designed to want to be together physically. It serves an emotional purpose- human contact and it continues the human race. It's programming that cannot be denied. Finding time for intimacy after childbirth can be difficult and you may feel self-conscious knowing there are ears on the other side of the wall. But I promise you, it's important for your kids to know you are intimate. What do they need to know? They need to see a peck on the cheek, a hug, a long kiss, cuddling. That's all they need to see. The rest is for you and your partner which brings me to my next point- Lock your door!

Curious minds will be waltzing in to check on you unless you lock the door. There may even be questions about what you were doing. Our blanket answer is we were loving each other with hugs and kisses. (that's when they are young) Once they know about sex, we don't have to explain any further. :-) When they complain about us being noisy, we respond, "Be glad we are still loving and hugging. It's a sign of a healthy family."

Teach your child the importance of knocking on a door. This may seem like an obvious thing to you, but it is not to them. You've probably noticed that your child does not understand personal space. They will freely be in your bubble- crawling over you, hugging you, interrupting you, sitting on your lap even when adult sized if you let them! If you are like I was as a new mom this was OK but, as time went on and social skills were expected, there were some embarrassing consequences of not teaching boundaries. For instance, you have a guest at the house who is using the bathroom and your 10-year-old barges in on them. Or you are changing your clothes and they stumble across you bare naked, or you are in a changing room in a store, and they fling open the curtain exposing you to everyone and asking loudly, "Why are you naked??" (true story!) Can you see what I mean?

And so the lesson must be taught. Modeling helps but that is not always the best way since many autistic minds are not the best observers. Practice does help. Show them how to knock and explain why. Explain that the closed door is a barrier that must be respected and that you will do the same for them. I always knock before entering my son's room to share in the process. If you don't have the ability to lock your door, teach them to watch for a sign on the door of your liking. It could be a picture of a hand in the stop position, an actual stop sign, a "do not disturb" sign or whatever works for nonreaders and readers.

Boundary tip #3 **Consider treating your bedroom as a sacred space.**

Do you sleep with your kids? It's ok to say yes but I want you to consider a few things.
Why do you sleep with them?
Is it the only way they can sleep?
Are you too lazy to go into their room if they need you?
Are you hoping to avoid sexual activity with your partner?

I want you to be honest with yourself about your answer.

There are mixed thoughts about the benefits of co-sleeping and sometimes it's a requirement of the culture or living conditions. If you have the opportunity to provide a separate sleeping space for your child, I want to encourage you to do it. Here's why. If you give away your most intimate space- your sleeping chamber- where you enter the most vulnerable state of REM and deep relaxation, when and where do you refuel? If you're worried your kids' feelings will be hurt when your bedroom is off limits, know that they will adjust. In the long run they will respect your space and expect you to respect theirs. They will gain the joy of having private time because you showed them how to appreciate it for themselves. Your bedroom should be a place to safely reflect your wishes in decor and atmosphere that best suits you. It should not be molded around a child's whims, full of unfolded laundry, centered around a TV, or used as a secondary playroom for your kids. It is a sacred space where you can escape, refuel, take downtime, reflect, dream, and in the end become a better person for your family. So now knowing that, where will your child sleep tonight? If you are trying to move them to their own room, it will be tricky but, with encouragement, and joyous feeling surrounding their new environment, it can happen. Just like your room, their room should be a reflection of them. Even if you hate the wall color they chose (my son chose black!) or they don't want wall decor or they need their head at the wrong end of the bed, respect that and give them ownership.

Family Craft- Construct some signs together that clearly communicate your boundaries. They can be funny or serious as long as the message is clear. Kids have been doing this for years (keep out, no girls allowed, etc.) so why not the grown-ups too?

Boundary tip #4 **Saying "No" as a positive habit**

How easily do you say "no"? Does it make you uncomfortable to refuse to do something for another? Do you feel guilt for wanting to take time for yourself? Do you share all your personal activities with those around you? Are your children constantly in your space because you let them?

As a woman, I bet you resonate with most of these. The compulsion to say yes and allow others to invade our private lives has been conditioned for many years. We are supposed to be providers, caretakers, listeners, chauffeurs, organizers, fundraisers, chefs, financiers, disciplinarians, maids, teachers, medics, and more. And this is just in your own home! If you are expected to or want to have a job outside of home too, you've taken on even more. As moms and professionals, our task list is long and exhaustive, but the biggest problem is ourselves. Few of us have been encouraged to set boundaries. Our family members don't tell us to set boundaries because they would miss out on all the wonderful things we do for them! Why would they want to change this? They don't keep asking and expecting because they are having a power trip, it's because we keep saying yes.

So why are your needs so important above and beyond the others? It is because if you are not in good shape to help, receive or give love to yourself, you are of no use to anyone. The quote from the airline safety speech- "put on your oxygen mask before helping others," is my mantra. It has helped me understand why saying "no" is sometimes the best way to care for others.

So, let's take a look at how we handle this with parenting. When I was a new mom, I gave all my time and energy to my child- Like most of us do. And I also could not understand the parents who actually put their own needs first. I saw them as selfish and uncaring. As time went on and I was getting run down and my son's autism symptoms were getting worse, I was noticing my ability to cope was also diminishing. It took some good soul searching to finally understand where I was failing myself. I was not putting on my oxygen mask first. So, I wanted to share with you a few bits of advice to reinforce the idea that self-care is necessary and not a reason for guilt or self-hatred or judging.

1. Every day, find some time to yourself. This can be a 10-minute meditation, a long hot bath, reading, a walk, crafting. Whatever brings you joy and separates you from the daily grind.

2. Make your rules clear. For instance, children will take every bit of space in your home that you give them- Including your bathroom! Until you make clear rules and establish boundaries, they will assume that your space is their space. So some spaces that should be sacred to you are the bathroom, a favorite chair in a private space, your garden, your home gym, bedroom or whatever space you can carve out just for yourself. And be sure the rules are expressed and posted with an easy to understand sign such as "Mom's Space," "Adults only" or even "Keep out" if you need to be that bold. If this concept really bothers you, teach your kids to appreciate their private space too. Then you will all have a common understanding of its value.

3. Get help. When I was a new mom, my son never slept. So as a result, I never slept. My husband had a day job so that

left me as the only provider. Except! I had babysitters and I was not too proud to use them. I hired a sitter to watch my son so I could take a nap. Yep! I really did! And boy did I sleep! I knew he was near but also safe so I could let go of my responsibilities and refuel. What ways can you get help? Laundry? Cooking? Cleaning? These all free you up to care for yourself.

4. Make an activity for you and your partner that does not allow the kids to be involved. You remember when you first met and you spent time together without distraction? That needs to continue. It's so important that you two still build memories that are only yours! This could be as simple as grabbing some to-go meal and eating at a park while the kids are at school or having a weekly movie night after they've gone to bed. It does not need to be involved or expensive but it does need to happen. When my son was 19 and living in a young adult community, my husband and I took a week in Hawaii and a week in England. It was amazing how fast we were able to reconnect and just have fun together!

5. And finally- keep in mind your priorities. As a school parent you will have all sorts of pressures put on you to be in band boosters, chaperone activities, PTA, etc. Before you say yes, ask yourself if it meets your mission. If the time after school with your kids is super important to you then keep that time sacred. Rethink how many activities they really need to be active in because it will impact you too. Invite the family to help with dinner preparations and make them a part of the household routine.

By saying "no" you are expressing self-love and the more love you make, the more you can share. And as a result, the more respect you will gain from colleagues, other parents and even your own kids.

Deep Dive-

When was the last time you gave yourself a compliment? Did you even realize that it is OK to do this? It's actually quite important! On a daily basis find a compliment that resonates with you such as "My hair is gorgeous today" or "I made a delicious dinner!" or "I'm a great mom!" Once you are comfortable with these you can dig deeper and say things like "I am loved" "I am important" "I am worthy." The more positive affirmations you say to yourself the more positive you will feel. And if you share affirmations with those around you, they will also resonate with positivity.

1. Write three affirmations that make you feel great right now.
2. Write three affirmations that you don't feel ready for now but could use in the future.
   Example: I am a woman of love and contentment. I am a woman of light and knowledge. I am worthy of all positive actions that come my way. I am ready to receive.
3. As much as you may struggle to love yourself, I guarantee that your child struggles even more. You can teach your child affirmations to combat negative self-talk but I find more

success if I speak it for my son. I read this affirmation to my son as he's falling to sleep at night.

> *"You are part of creation*
> *Just like the tree*
> *outside your window*
> *just like your cats and dogs*
> *And you are so deeply loved*
> *And supported by Life and Creation*
> *because you are part of it.*
> *Just that you are alive means*
> *You belong and are valued."*
>
> *-Susan Morse*

And here's a reminder of the 3 tools you deserve to set up for your sanity:

Start with an affirmation such as "I am deserving" and then
1. Communicate your emotional needs
2. Find a private space for yourself
3. Just say "No"

Love Notes to Myself

You Were Made For This

Rebecca Jeffreys

Chapter 7
Self-Compassion, Self-Care and Perspective Taking

"If your compassion does not involve yourself, you are incomplete"
-The Buddha

Compassion is a difficult emotion to master. Merriam Webster Dictionary shares this definition: "sympathetic consciousness of others distress together with a desire to alleviate it." When I finally understood compassion, it felt like I found the greatest tool for emotional mastery ever revealed to me. I had been reading about compassion in Buddhist writings and other lofty writings, but it really took an a-ha moment for me to finally get it! A good deal of my training to become a competitive classical musician centered around critiquing others' abilities. Now this is a valuable tool for self-evaluation, but it can also be very destructive. Comparing oneself to others on a regular basis is not a recommended practice. Out of self-protection of the ego, I started cataloging people according to their abilities as musicians. I also had determined that if they did not play well, they were not taking their craft seriously and therefore, they were not worth my time. Just think of all the wonderful people I never got to know because they did not meet my standard!

Jump ahead 10 years after college and I was finding myself struggling with personalities that were stressing me out. I often found myself thinking: "I can't deal with them. Too much drama and so needy!" Never once did it occur to me to think differently about them. I was still putting them in my black and white categories of capable or not capable. In my head it was obvious they were incapable. I am glad to say that eventually all the reading I had been doing eventually sank in! It was not they who had to change, it was me! And so I found another way to look at things. I started asking questions such as, "Are they struggling right now? Is there some way I can help? Am I misunderstanding their situation?" I can't even begin to tell you how much lightness I felt when I changed my perspective.

This enlightenment came at a key point in my life too. I was just beginning to see that I was raising a child with challenges. I had a couple of choices to make about how I reacted to parenting situations. I could blow up at my child because he was behaving badly, oddly, crazy (your choice) or I could sit back and ask, "What is really going on here? Is he anxious? Is he misunderstanding the situation? Did I make an incorrect assumption about his understanding of what's going on? Is my expectation too vague or abstract?" When I opened myself to these questions, answers would arrive. My parenting became more intuitive and compassionate. By asking questions that helped him get to the answers he was having trouble finding, we cooperatively arrived at a solution which made both of us much happier!

I want to remind you to put your oxygen mask on before helping others. Growing up I was conditioned to believe that everyone else came before me. Self-care was never a topic of discussion beyond personal hygiene. So in my head, putting my needs ahead of others was a big no-no. Did anyone ever really tell me this? Probably not but it was the conclusion I made by watching my family and the lessons I learned at church. I'm telling you now, YOU need to come first!

Your body and your mind are vessels. They were put on this Earth to yes, serve others, but they are useless if they are not properly cared for. By putting your oxygen mask on first, you are guaranteeing you can help needier people such as children. So how do we include self-care when so much of our time is spent caring for a special needs child? It won't happen on its own.

Deep Dive

1. Read the chapter about boundaries (Chapter 6) and put things into position for you to succeed.
2. Find time for yourself to refuel. You'd be amazed how powerful 10 minutes of meditation or quiet thinking can power you up! There are hundreds of free guided meditations on-line. A quick catnap, time with a favorite novel or magazine, walking, gardening, scrapbooking. I used to watch incense burn before bed as the motion was calming and helped me decompress for a good night's sleep. This is not being selfish. It's being a caretaker for yourself so you can help others. I'll keep reminding you of that! Personal time is super important and should happen daily if possible. Waiting for the right moment is just going to build resentment because that moment won't happen unless you make it.
3. You remember getting your nails and hair done and how good you felt afterward? or for the athletes, that time you broke your own personal record, or for the writers, that time you saw your name on the cover of your first book? I bet

you can immediately revisit the sensation of pride and joy you felt in your own accomplishment. When was the last time you felt that? If you can't even remember, it's time to revisit YOU! It's so easy to be identified as so and so's mom, but you are so much more than that! Reinvesting in you as an individual is so important and good for your overall well-being. Can you think of one thing today that makes you unique? I rediscovered horseback riding in my 40's. It really was a game changer for my mental health! I found an activity that required my full attention, that was comfortably challenging and extremely rewarding. Finally, I could talk and <u>think</u> about something other than parenting. Whatever investment you make in yourself it will be the most important investment ever because you will once again refuel yourself and in turn be able to better serve others.

4. Some gifts you can give yourself - Make a chore list for the family, hire someone to clean your house, order dinner delivery, schedule your personal time, hire an aid, go away by yourself for a weekend, take a spa day, take a hike, take a class, visit a museum, see a play, craft, go out on a date, have

some tea, pick some flowers, tell your partner what you need, dream! You need this!!

You Were Made For This

Here's a gift from my family to yours:

Grandma Smock's Green Magic Love Tea

1 tbsp of each:

    licorice root to boost desire

    sesame seeds to comfort the soul

    dried rosemary for remembrance

    lemon grass to incite lust

    dried nettle leaf for vitamin C. Always helpful

    Dried orange peel for a sunny outlook

1 tsp each:

    powdered ginger

    cinnamon

    fennel seeds for sensuous aroma

    gotu kola to boost sexual appetite

Grind all ingredients with mortar and pestle

Pour 1 pint boiling water over mixture, cover and simmer for 20 minutes. Strain through cheesecloth. Add honey and serve hot or cold. Lovers should share the drink together for best results.

Rebecca Jeffreys

You Were Made For This

Chapter 8
Celebrate!

Social media can be so cruel. Your friends are posting about their kids getting into their favorite colleges or passing their driving exam or going to prom and you are sitting there struggling to find something to celebrate. Comparing your situation to others is certain death to your self-esteem. There are few things I want you to realize about their posts.

1. They only reveal the good stuff. Despite having typical kids, they also face challenges.
2. They are just as insecure as you are. Seeking applause and approval on Facebook is not a requirement, it is a plea for attention.
3. You are not required to post anything personal on social media. Really, your personal life is none of their business. It's become commonplace to broadcast our lives but it's really not a requirement of human social norms. The few times I have posted about my son, I have always asked his

permission. Remember, your kids are people who deserve privacy too.

Well, you may be feeling some relief from this news about social media. However, I do want you to still celebrate your success and wins and yes! You do have them!

Raising an atypical kid calls for a change in mindset when it comes to recognizing successes. If you are looking to your own childhood rites of passage markers for success, they probably won't work for your kid. It took me a long time to come to terms with this! But once I did, I saw my son for who he is, not who I hoped he'd be.

So, what does success look like in my home? When he was little, getting through a day without a rant was a grand success. Finding ways to help with his gut issues- HUGE success! Seeing his gorgeous artwork come home from school. Score!! In high school the successes we celebrated were: seeing him advocate for his needs, seeing joy in his face when going to school, seeing him let himself into our home with a key and managing the dogs until I got home from work- priceless! I'm sure you noticed there's no academic celebration here. His grades were fine but really not of much importance for us. He has a gift for acing standardized tests and even though he won a scholarship to the state colleges, he couldn't use it. So we changed our focus. We took pressure off of him to try athletics (rules are hard and his low muscle tone makes it difficult to do any sports), we removed academic pressure and we let him explore other options. As a result he found his strengths and we celebrated! Did we ever brag? Of course! To grandparents and aunts and uncles and close friends who knew how hard these successes were for him and us.

One of our biggest celebrations came when we enrolled him in a gap year program after high school. While he tried his best to share an apartment and work as an intern, my husband and I took a trip by ourselves. We had a fantastic time and for the first time in a very long time, we were giddy! That was a very long awaited and well-deserved celebration of us!

Deep Dive:

What can you celebrate? There is no "importance meter" assigned to this question.
Did your child put on their own socks today? Celebrate!!!
Did you get some time to yourself? Celebrate!!!
Did your child show initiative and take care of their own self-care? You know the drill… **Celebrate!**

So, what does your celebration look like?

Journals are a great place to keep track of these victories.

When you're feeling less than successful, review your victories for a pick me up. You'll see all that you have accomplished and realize that there will be more!

Have a once-a-month celebration with moms with similar kids.

We really do need to cheer each other on!

Have a party at home with the family. Did you hit a big milestone?

Make a big deal about it! Balloons, food, dance party.

Whatever feels festive to you is the right thing to do.

For us, a big milestone was the first time my son sat at the Thanksgiving table. He could finally manage the noise and chaos. Woot Woot!! My husband and I had a personal dance party over that one!

And finally, I want you to celebrate YOU! Look at what you have accomplished. You brought an amazing child into this world who will teach us about ourselves and help us become better humans. You have done research and found the best services for them. You have cooked their favorite foods and taken them to appointments. You have stayed up late helping them with their anxiety. You have held a job, managed a household and been a caretaker. And somehow you found more of yourself to share with your spouse and other children. For these reasons and more, you are a superhero. I recognize your strengths, your successes and failures, your imperfections, your frustrations, and your tears.

YOU WERE MADE FOR THIS AND YOU ARE THE BEST PERSON FOR THE JOB!

Rebecca Jeffreys

A parting thought by Rudolph Steiner

A Verse for Our Time

We must eradicate from the soul
All fear and terror of what comes towards
man out of the future.
We must acquire serenity
In all feelings and sensations about the future.
We must look forward with absolute equanimity
To everything that may come.
And we must think only that whatever comes
Is given to us by a world-directive full of wisdom.
It is part of what we must learn in this age,
namely, to live out of pure trust,
Without any security in existence.
Trust in the ever-present help
Of the spiritual world.
Truly nothing else will do
If our courage is not to fail us.
And let us seek the awakening from within ourselves
Every morning and every evening.

You Were Made For This

Appendix:

Choosing a Therapeutic or Special Needs School

If you have reached a crossroads and need to consider sending your child to a special needs or therapeutic school here are a few things to inquire about. I would encourage you to seek places that match your parenting philosophy. In other words, how would you handle these situations at home. Three aspects that were really important for me was understanding their policy on restraining (I did not want this), life skills (yes!) and how they would meet state minimums for academic requirements. If the campus was beautiful and welcoming, that was even better! One school that we visited had such a terrible setting that my son was asking to leave about 10 minutes after we arrived. I had to agree with him. There is no such thing as a perfect school but if you keep communication open and continue to advocate you can make for a positive experience.

Check on these items:

Restraining techniques or other extreme methods for control

Academics (diploma versus certificate)

Life skills

Extended day program

Post high school job training programs

Job training for those with developmental disabilities

Art, music etc.

Clinicians available. How many clinicians and how often do they meet your child? Are they available during a crisis?

Do they have a "quiet" room for de-escalating or recovery from too much stimulation?

What is the method for evacuations if a child is becoming dangerous?

How and whom is your point of contact?

What are cell phone rules?

Is there transportation available? What are the guidelines used there? Is there an assistant on the bus?

Is there on-campus medical staff? Can your child get their medications while at school?

What are the cafeteria guidelines?

How do they handle food allergies?

Do they provide in classroom sensory tools?
Is there an occupational therapist or speech therapist on staff?

Do they offer therapeutic horseback riding?

What do kids do after graduation?

What grade levels are served?
How often do you meet with the special education team?

Do they include physical fitness?

Are there community building activities?

Do they take day trips?

Is there homework?

What is their bullying policy?

Does school go year-round?

How do they handle kids who bolt or wander?

Do they follow HIPAA Policy practices? This would mean that you may not ever meet any other parents and your child may not be able to have playdates at your house. This worked out fine for us as my son just wanted to rest after getting home. He had enough socializing at school.

If you need to consider residential schools, you'll want to know this too:

Can your child come home on weekends?

Can you meet the staff?

Can you contact staff?

Can you call your child?

Can you visit the dorms?

How do they handle conflict?

Is the staff trained in working with this particular population?

And finally- What does it cost? Always try to get your local school district to cover this first.

What to do with all the paperwork:

As you progress through life with your special needs child, you will collect quite a bit of paperwork. It will be tempting to throw these out as time goes by, but you will need to refer to reports all the way back to the beginning.

You should expect reports from:

    neuropsychologists

    The special education department

    speech therapist

    occupational therapist

    physical therapist

    psychologist

    psychiatrist

    Independent Education Plan (IEP)

    504 Plan

    Your state's disability services

Some forms are more important than others and will be referenced again and again.

I suggest you combine your IEPs, neuropsychology reports and school reports all in one binder for quick reference. Or at the very least, make a digital file and keep them all in a folder.

These forms come in handy when applying for services or even for legal battles. They are especially helpful when formulating your child's IEP and helps the school know what services to provide. Even after graduation, you will need these records to apply for SSI (Supplemental Security Income) and disability services.

Glossary

This list of terms are words you will encounter in this book and/or through the years while raising your child.

Affirmation- A positive statement directed at oneself for the purpose of encouraging a positive behavior.

Applied Behavior Analysis (ABA) therapy- A therapy used to encourage helpful behaviors and discourage unhelpful ones. Can help with language and communication skills, improve attention, focus, social skills, memory, and academics.

Apraxia of speech- associated with autism. Child has trouble getting their tongue and mouth cavity to form basic sounds of speech.

ASD- Autism Spectrum Disorder. Includes several conditions: autistic disorder, pervasive developmental disorder not otherwise specified (PDD-NOS), and Asperger syndrome.

Circular thinking- an illogical, repetitive thought process that cannot be broken. also see: perseverate, rumination and fixation.

Craniosacro therapy- a gentle massage of the head and neck to relieve compression of the vertebrae in order to treat neurology. This is not an autism cure.

DD- Developmental Disabilities are a group of conditions due to an impairment in physical, learning, language, or behavior areas that usually last for a lifetime. Autism is a developmental disability.

Echolalia- the process of repeating words or phrases over and over.

EFT Emotional Freedom Technique (or psychological acupressure)- The process of tapping one one's forehead, temples, chest and wrists in order to release stress or anxiety.

EIBI: Early Intensive Behavioral Intervention. 20-40 hours per week of individualized instruction for ASD kids younger than 4.

Executive functioning- the mind's ability to organize its thoughts and actions in a productive way. i.e. Set and keep a schedule or do homework and turn it in on time.

Fixation- the inability to release a repetitive thought.

Flat affect- an autistic human's inability to show emotion in their verbal or facial expressions.

GAD- general anxiety disorder.

Hyperfocus- Intense interest in one activity to the point of blocking out external stimuli. Can last for a long period of time.

IEP- Individualized education plan devised by your school and you to best make accommodations for your child. Requires goal setting and record of measurable growth.

Impulsive- reacting and acting out without thinking about consequences.

Intrusive ideation- unwanted, distressing thoughts that cannot be released. Often illogical and formed as a result of traumatic experiences.

ISP- individual support team provided by your state to help your adult child establish goals and seek employment or higher education within their abilities.

Leaky Gut- the inability for the lining of the intestines to protect the body from toxins. Not generally regarded as a medical diagnosis.

MDD- major depressive disorder.

Modulation- the process of self-regulating physical responses to external stimuli.

Neuropsychological evaluation- a lengthy exam given by a psychologist to determine your child's diagnosis, school needs and therapies.

Obsessive compulsive disorder (OCD)- an anxiety disorder in which the person feels compelled to react to uncontrollable and repetitive behaviors or compulsive thoughts.

Occupational therapy- a practice that helps individuals with daily tasks such as chores, writing and physical fitness.

Pediatric psychopharmacologist- a trained and certified doctor who best helps determine medicines for a child's mental health.

Perseverate- another form of fixation, circular thinking and rumination.

Proprioception- sensory information sent through muscles and bones telling the body how much movement it needs to complete a task and where it is in space.

Psychiatrist- a doctor trained and certified to prescribe medications.

Rumination- obsessive thoughts concerning extreme, recurring ideas or concepts that get in the way of daily activities and thought processes.

SAT- college board test to check for college readiness.

Sensory integration- the body's ability to properly receive and process information through the 5 senses.

Sensory Modality- the way in which a person receives information through their senses. (proprioceptive, vestibular, visual, tactile, auditory, gustatory, olfactory)

Slow processing disorder- the inability for the brain to digest information and react upon it at the expected speed. Can result in delayed reactions to questions.

Special Needs Advocate- a professional familiar with special needs rules and laws who can assist you in getting services for your child.

Stimming- self-stimulatory behaviors (e.g., flapping arms over and over, hitting head, or spinning) in order to reduce anxiety or process information.

Suicidal ideation- obsessive thoughts about suicide.

Therapeutic horseback riding- a form of Equine facilitated learning which helps with sensory integration, physical strength, emotional and social interaction. It can work in accordance with IEP. To find professional teachers use a barn with certified PATH International teachers.

Vestibular input- a sensory channel that depends on direction, position or movement of the head.

504 Plan- an education plan that recognizes a disability and calls for accommodations. Does not require records of measurable growth.

Additional resources:

National Suicide Prevention Lifeline 800-273-8255

Hours: Available 24 hours. Languages: English, Spanish.

Domestic Abuse Hotline- Call 1.800.799.SAFE (7233)

Child abuse hotline- 1-800-4-A-Child (1-800-422-4453)

Crisis text- 741741 to speak to a crisis counselor

National Autism Association - 877.622.2884

naa@nationalautism.org

About The Author

Rebecca Jeffreys, The Autism Mom, is a coach for moms who are raising kids on the spectrum. In her previous life, she was a classical musician. Her years of teaching and collaborating has given her skills for listening, patience and building trust.

She offers parenting blogs on her website and has been published on TheMighty.com and CentralMassMoms.com website.

Rebecca offers group and private coaching, and she is also the host of the podcast, "The Caretakers with Rebecca Jeffreys" which can be found on your favorite platforms.

For more information and to schedule a discovery session visit www.sproutinghealthyfamilies.com.

You Were Made For This

Rebecca Jeffreys is also available to be a guest on podcasts. Contact her directly at: rebecca@sproutinghealthyfamilies.com

About The Illustrator

Jeffrey Hoover holds a Ph.D. in Fine Arts (Composition and Interdisciplinary Fine Arts) from Texas Tech University, as well as an M.M. in Composition and Musicology and B.A.Sc., in Music Education from Ball State University.

Photo credit: Chris Hartlove

You can learn more about Hoover's combination of art and music through his website:

https://jeffreyhooverart.wixsite.com/mysite

Made in the USA
Columbia, SC
04 May 2021

36496256R10080